Dear Hope... Love, Grandma

Hilda Abramson Hurwitz
and
Hope R. Wasburn

Edited by
Mara H. Wasburn

Alef Design Group
Los Angeles

Library of Congress Cataloging-in-Publication Data
Hurwitz, Hilda Abramson, 1902–1991.
   Dear Hope—Love, Grandma / Hilda Abramson Hurwitz and Hope
Wasburn ; edited by Mara H. Wasburn.
         p.   cm.
   ISBN 1-881283-03-8 : $13.95
      1. Hurwitz, Hilda Abramson, 1902–1991—Correspondence—Juvenile
literature. 2. Wasburn, Hope, 1978–   —Correspondence—Juvenile
literature. 3. Jews—Missouri—Saint Louis—Correspondence—Juvenile
Literature. 4. Children of immigrants—Missouri—Saint Louis—
Correspondence—Juvenile literature.   [1. Grandmothers. 2. Jews—
Biography. 3. Immigrants. 4. Letters. 5. Children's writings.] I. Wasburn,
Hope, 1978–   . II. Waburn, Mara H., 1941–   . III. Title.
   F474.S29J54   1993
   972.8ꞌ6604ꞌ092—dc20   93-2213
                                                                    CIP
                                                                    AC

Published by Alef Design Group

Alef Design Group
4423 Fruitland Avenue
Los Angeles, California 90058
(213) 582-1200

Dedication

To my indomitable mother, Hilda Abramson Hurwitz (1902–1991), whose heartwarming stories of her close-knit family so enriched my childhood, and to my daughter, Hope, whose interest in those stories has given her Grandma a kind of immortality.

Dear Hope…Love, Grandma

In 1987, when my daughter Hope was in the third grade, she participated in a class project to exchange letters with senior citizens. The project was designed to occupy the children's summer in a productive way, and to help them learn about everyday life when these older Americans were young—something they could not learn from history books. Alas, Hope's designated correspondent never answered her letters.

Seeing her disappointment, I reminded her that she had an eighty-three-year-old grandma who would be delighted to write to her, and who had a wealth of stories to share. So Hope sent her grandma the following letter:

June 10, 1987

Dear Grandma,

We are sort of going to be pen pals. I had a pen pal in a old peoples' home in Davis Manor, but I guess she forgot to write back. I think you'll make a much better one. When you write to me, please write a story of your childhood, or about anyone in your family. I hope you like the stationery. I drew it by myself. Please write back soon.

Love,

Hope

Thus began a long and somewhat surprising exchange of letters between Hope and her grandma. Very soon, Hope and I began to see that what was emerging was more than just a class project. The stories revealed a charming picture of a widow's struggles to raise her five children in an unfamiliar land, to make them feel secure, to give them her values of courage, love, faith in God, and loyalty to one another, and to provide them with a sense of humor to see them through the difficult times ahead.

It then occurred to us that without Hope's class project, my mother's stories and memories would have died with her. How many other memories, how many other stories have already vanished from the face of the earth, with no one to preserve them?

It is our hope that the publication of this book will encourage other children to embark on similar projects with their own grandparents while they are still alive. They, too, have much to tell. What they need is someone to listen.

Mara Wasburn

DEAR HOPE...

LOVE, GRANDMA

Dear Grandma,

We are sort of going to be pen pals....

Dear Hope,

Whatever her reason for not answering your letter, I am grateful to the old lady in the nursing home, because now you and I can be pen pals instead. Perhaps in each letter you can tell me what you are doing, and I can share some stories of my childhood in St. Louis in the early 1900s.

Because this is summer and you are not in school, I'll write about the time my brother Harry (who was about three and a half years older than I) and I were undecided about what we were going to do with our time. Our mother—your great grandma—suggested that we plant a garden. She told us how to plant corn and how to pull up the weeds. She told us to water the ground and how to care for the corn. It did not, however, occur to her that we would not know how to proceed from there. She had grown up in a little village in Poland where *everybody* knew about planting and caring for crops. How could she guess that we would be so excited when we saw the silk at the top of each ear of corn that we would pull most of it off to see if the cobs had any kernels? Of course, not only did the cobs have no kernels, they never grew any kernels. We learned the hard way. Mamma said *everybody* makes mistakes, so we felt better.

When you answer this letter, do let me know how Aaron, Leah and you are spending your summer. I'd be interested in comparing your summer with our summers of long ago.

Love,

Grandma

My brother Harry and I were undecided about what we were going to do with our time.

June 19, 1987

Dear Grandma,

That was a very funny story that you wrote about the corn. Did it ever grow at all? Do you know where I put your letter? Leah helped me make a little sort of folder out of some cardboard. I covered it with wallpaper so it will look good. Your letter looks very nice in it. Please write soon.

Your pen pal,

Hope

June 23, 1987

Dear Hope,

Your letter came today. How nice of Leah to help you make a cardboard folder to keep my letters in, and how creative of you to cover it with wallpaper. I am saving your letters, too!

To answer your question, the corn stalks did grow tall—very tall. They did produce ears of corn, but the cobs did not have any kernels on them. That's the effect that pulling the silk off had on our crop.

One winter when I was about seven years old, we had a guest. My Uncle Lazar, who had not seen his brother for over thirty years, came for a visit. Mamma recognized him at once, but Papa did not. Uncle Lazar was over six feet tall and knew how to stand even taller. He wore a beaver coat and a beaver hat. He lived in Maine, where the winters are bitter cold, and where he owned a successful business.

Papa was the opposite. He was *not* especially tall, and he was *not* interested in making money. He was a rabbi—an orthodox rabbi—a scholar, and a brilliant speaker. In those days, Orthodox rabbis received no salaries from their congregations as they do now.

The brothers and Mamma had a wonderful time reliving their memories of Poland and catching up on the years in between. My older sisters—Sophie and Sarah—had a wonderful time going shopping with this uncle, who didn't care what anything cost.

All I remember of his brief visit is that with Sophie and Sarah's help, everybody in the family received something that he or she needed and something that he or she wanted. To this day I can still remember the beautiful dark blue, double-breasted winter coat my Uncle Lazar bought me, and even more clearly, the magnificent doll—the kind I had never seen before.

It was big—but not too big. It had a beautiful china face and china hands and feet, and a kidskin body. Its clothes—in all shades of pink—defy description. I *loved* it, I slept with it, I ate with it, and I lived with it.

Months later, I don't know how it happened, but taking the doll off Mamma's high bed, I dropped it. To my horror, the face shattered. My screams brought everybody at once, but even Mamma realized the hopelessness of the situation. It was just too costly to replace.

All the same, my sisters did try to find another doll as much like the one I had loved as they could find. They returned with a lovely *unbreakable* doll. Sarah, who was a gifted seamstress and made as many of my clothes as she could, outfitted the doll with several changes, and I learned to love it, too.

Love,

Grandma

"My older sisters—Sophie and Sarah....

June 27, 1987

Dear Grandma,

Did I forget to tell you about our earthquake right here in Indiana? It happened only a few weeks ago. I'm glad I wasn't writing your letter then. Do you know what? People's dogs were jumping around and barking ten minutes before the earthquake occurred. Is a kidskin doll a rag doll? You said it was unbreakable. I don't have many dolls with yellow hair. Did she have real hair? Some of my dolls do. What was the second doll you had made out of? It must have been pretty unbreakable. Was it a rag doll? Please write back soon.

Your pen pal,

Hope

P.S. I put your letter in the notebook with the other one.

July 7, 1987

Dear Hope,

Did you feel the earthquake in Lafayette? I find it
interesting that people's dogs barked for ten minutes
before the quake. Dogs must have an inner barometer.

I should have realized that you wouldn't know what a
kidskin doll is. Kidskin is leather, and it felt as soft as a
person's skin. If I had a sense of history, I would have
kept that doll, so that your mother—when she was a
little girl—and her little girls would have known what
kind of dolls children who were loved played with many
years ago.

I do not have a clear memory of Papa. He died when I
was very young. It was against his religious beliefs to
have a picture taken, and that is too bad. Everyone said
that he had a sensitive face, fine features, and clear,
piercing eyes.

Like him, Mamma was very religious. When I read *The
Little House in the Big Woods*, I was amazed at how
much Sunday at the Ingalls house resembled our
Sabbath when I was growing up. All the baking and

cooking were done on Friday. By seven o'clock on Friday morning there were three large h̲allahs, three tiny h̲allahs for the younger children (Rosie, Harry and me), and a coffee cake cooling on the table. The house was cleaned from top to bottom, and the seven brass candlesticks (one for each member of the family) were polished until they gleamed. The table was covered with a special white Shabbat tablecloth, and the candlesticks placed on a tray in the center. It all looked so lovely.

Although I grew up many years after Laura Ingalls Wilder, a woman still had to work hard to build a fire in a cookstove. At sundown on Friday night all work stopped. From then until sundown on Saturday there was no cooking, no fixing a fire in the stove or adding coal, no writing or sewing or any manner of work. In the winter, a non–Jewish boy would come in and add coal.

Although lighting the gas is not the work that building a fire in the coal stove was, to this day I do not cook on the Sabbath. Also, I cannot bring myself to knit or sew or even write, unless the writing is absolutely necessary. That is what my Mamma did, and that is what I do, because it really is a wonderful idea to have a day that is entirely different from all other days.

Last Saturday—the Fourth of July, my mind kept dwelling on how different it was from the Fourth of July when I was a child. My sister Sarah told me that when she and Sophie were little, Papa kept them indoors the whole day so that they wouldn't be harmed by the fireworks. BUT, when my sister Rosie, my brother Harry and I were little, things were different. We all had fireworks, and we all made as much noise as possible. Those kinds of fireworks are against the law now because they are dangerous. All over the country there were reports of people being hurt, but none of us was ever hurt. We were just lucky. But we did have fun.

Love,

Grandma

We all had fireworks, and we all made as much noise as possible.

July 14, 1987

Dear Grandma,

We are going to California! I will have my birthday dinner in Kansas, I think. I am having swim lessons every day, the water is cold. Our instructor is nice. I can almost swim now. By the time you get this letter, I will probably be able to swim. We *really* liked your story. I can't wait for another.

Love,

Your pen pal,

Hope

July 18, 1987

Dear Hope,

Your mamma did, indeed, tell me that you are going to California. How excited you must be! I hope you have time to swim there.

My mamma was a happy person, a person with a great sense of humor. She laughed often, and when she laughed, she didn't make one sound. When she told a funny story, all of a sudden she started to laugh and shake all over, so that you didn't understand one word of what she was saying for quite a while.

Mamma needed that sense of humor, because her life was not easy. After Papa died, Mamma had to support her five children alone. She had a grocery store and was up by five o'clock every morning so she would have time to recite her prayers before breakfast. Then she hurried off to work. When she came home at night she was always very tired. After dinner she would sit down in her favorite chair in the living room until she fell asleep. She said that she slept much better sitting in that chair than she did in her bed. Of course, when she awoke about midnight, she would go to bed.

What Mamma enjoyed most of all was to have either my sister Rosie or me comb her hair while she was relaxing in her chair. One wintry night I offered to comb her hair. I was about nine years old. I decided to try what I had been wanting to try for weeks. We had a black laundress who came every Monday and washed our clothes. In 1911, of course, there were no automatic washing machines. It was an all-day, backbreaking job. We loved having Martha come because we enjoyed her stories. Now and then she brought her little five-year-old granddaughter with her. Her granddaughter had her short hair combed into about fifty tiny braids. Each little braid had a tiny little ribbon that held it together at the end. I *loved* the way it looked.

On that night, I decided I would comb Mamma's hair just that way. So I cut a string into little pieces. It took me about an hour to make all those braids. Mamma had fallen asleep just as I had begun to comb her hair, and she was still sound asleep when I finished and went to bed.

The next morning I heard her tell my sister Sophie that at first she couldn't imagine what had happened to her hair. When she looked in the mirror and saw all of these little braids, she said that she laughed and laughed. She was still laughing when she told the story. She said it took her almost half an hour to take those little braids apart!

Love,

Grandma

P.S. Have a good trip!

She laughed often, and when she laughed, she didn't make one sound.

August 13, 1987

Dear Grandma,

Thank you so much for the birthday money. I bought a beautiful bracelet made of gold, copper, and silver. I can't describe it, but you will see it when you visit. I also bought a four-inch wooden Mexican Indian doll (measured with Grandpa's measurer) with the tiniest papoose on its back. It is only one inch. With Aunt Sarah's money I bought her a child, and I will draw pictures of them for you to look at.

Next time you write, please tell me some of the stories I know, like the time you ate a whole jar of peanut butter, or when you put everybody's shoes under their pillows. I think I have a doll that is a little like the one you broke, but mine's *much* smaller.

Love,

Your 9-year-old granddaughter,

Hope W.

P.S. I loved California!

August 17, 1987

Dear Hope,

I'm glad you had a good vacation. When I come to Lafayette you must tell me all about it.

I didn't dream that you wanted me to write stories you already knew! I was trying to avoid them.

When my sister Sarah and her husband Jake were just married, they moved to a small town called Pittsburg, Kansas. There were only a few stores there, and those stores did not have a great variety of things. So Jake got a catalogue from Montgomery Ward in Chicago. That store carried *everything*.

In the second summer of their marriage, which must have been in 1915, they sent me a train ticket to visit them for the entire summer. I was in seventh heaven! I had ridden on the train only once before in my life, and that was a ride that lasted only about thirty minutes. This was a long trip for a child to take, and Mamma had given the conductor strict instructions that he was to keep me on the train until my big sister arrived. You may be sure that she was there.

Anyway, before I had even left St. Louis, Sarah and Jake had sent an order to Montgomery Ward for peanut butter. They knew I had never tasted it and were positive I would enjoy it. They had never ordered peanut butter before and had no idea how much five pounds would be in quantity. A huge keg came; a keg big enough to feed a large family. Well, they were certainly right about my liking it.

I couldn't get my fill. I liked it on bread but *loved* it by the spoonful. Every time I went by the pantry I would take a tablespoonful of it. But the first time was the funniest.

Peanut butter, when I was a child, was not the peanut butter we buy today. Now it is smooth and easily swallowed. In those days peanut butter was made of freshly ground peanuts. If you took too much of it in your mouth at once, it stuck to your tongue and the roof of your mouth so that you couldn't swallow at once! It's a wonder that I didn't turn against it the first time I took a large spoonful of it. There I stood, almost choking, unable to call or say a word. But no, I did not let that keep me from eating almost the entire five pounds by the tablespoonful. I simply had learned how to handle it. However, by the end of summer, I had had my fill. Twenty or more years passed before I could stand to taste it again!

Today I have returned to liking peanut butter. I still prefer to fill a tablespoon and eat it as I did all those years ago.

Love,

Grandma

...Sarah and Jake had sent an order to Montgomery Ward for peanut butter.

August 21, 1987

Dear Grandma,

It certainly is hard to believe that you actually ate *five pounds* of peanut butter. I bet you got sick! Why didn't you know better than to put your shoes under the pillow? How old were you then? And what did everybody say when they got into bed? Please write me about it next time.

Your pen pal,

Hope

August 25, 1987

Dear Hope,

You are right, of course. It is hard to believe that a twelve-year-old, who was old enough to know better, could have eaten *five pounds* of peanut butter. You must remember, though, that I didn't eat it all in one day or even one week. I ate it in about eight weeks, but even then that was far from wise.

My oldest sister, Sophie, was the one who took care of the three younger children while Mamma was at her grocery store. Now Sophie had a rule, everybody must take care of his own things. There must be a place for everything, and it must be put there when you are not using it. In that way, there would never be much to clean up.

The summer before she was to be married, however, she decided that she ought to earn some money with which to buy her trousseau (things like sheets, towels, tablecloths, cooking utensils—everything she would need to furnish a home of her own). So she found work in an office and still managed to keep the house neat and clean.

One morning everybody but Mamma (who always left early for work) overslept, so nobody could put anything away. Sophie told Harry and me that she would give us a quarter if we would clean the house, because the man she was going to marry was coming to take her out to dinner. By the time she would get home from work, she would just have enough time to change her clothes, and she certainly didn't want him to find the house in a mess.

Now a quarter was a lot of money in those days. If we sat in the balcony, Harry and I were young enough to get *two* tickets for the movies for fifteen cents, and still have a nickel each to get a bag of candy! So we got to work. It was easy to wash the dishes, sweep the floors and dust the furniture. We put the dirty clothes in the hamper. But where should we put the shoes? We finally decided to put each person's shoes under his pillow. Then we ate an early dinner by ourselves and left for the movies.

The house looked lovely when Sophie came home. However, when she changed her clothes and looked for her best shoes, they were nowhere to be found. She looked everywhere she could think of. By this time she was absolutely furious. Finally it grew so late that she simply had to wear her old shoes. Not until she got home that night and went to bed did she discover where her good shoes were.

It has been such a long time since I thought of that summer that I may have left out some of the things I told your Mamma when she was a little girl. My Mamma always laughed when she even thought of what we children had done. Later, Sophie saw the humor of it and laughed, too, because she could never stay angry long.

Love,

Grandma

It is hard to believe that a twelve-year-old...could have eaten five pounds of peanut butter.

August 28, 1987

Dear Grandma,

That story was an especially good one. It is the best story you have written yet. Please write more about when you were little in your next letter. It is very interesting! I hope you get this letter!

Love,

Hope

Dear Hope,

I am so happy that you liked the story about the shoes under the pillow. We weren't trying to hide them, you understand. We just couldn't figure out where to put them.

That story reminded me of another one. We children knew that two times a year we got new shoes: right before school started in September, and again before the Passover holidays. They weren't just bought for us. We picked them out ourselves. Sophie made those days special days.

One year, when I was about eight, I selected a lovely pair of shoes. At least I thought the shoes were lovely, until about four weeks later I noticed that *all* the little girls were wearing shoes the likes of which I had never seen. They had black patent-leather bottoms, red or white leather uppers, and a wide two-inch band of black leather around the top (all shoes were high in those days). Down the front of those

shoes dangled a tassel. I *loved* them and envied every
little girl that owned a pair.

I knew there was no use asking Mamma if I could
have a pair. Money was scarce in our house. We
always had what we needed, but there was no money
to spare, and having a second pair of shoes when
they weren't needed would have been a waste. I did
confide to my sister Sophie how I now hated the ones
I wore, but Sophie said we were not to let Mamma
know about my being unhappy.

In about November I became ill with what is now
called the flu. Day after day the doctor came to the
house, but day after day I remained the same.

One day Sophie told Mamma about my wanting
those shoes so much. Mamma decided that maybe a
pair of those shoes would do what medicine could
not.

When I awoke from my nap at about five o'clock,
there, next to my bed, was a box. I was afraid to open
it for fear it would *not* be what it looked like, but it
was. There inside the tissue paper were the most
beautiful black and red shoes I had ever seen in my
whole life. And each shoe had not *one* tassel but *two*!
Of course, I had to try them on. They fit perfectly, and
they were the right medicine, because from that

moment I began to improve. It wasn't long before I was able to wear them to school.

I know that you and Aaron and Leah will be happy when school starts. The end of summer is always the most difficult time to get through. At least, I used to think so.

Love,

Grandma

September 6, 1987

Dear Grandma,

School started and I have nice teacher. I am in the fourth grade. My reading book is called *Gateways*. Did you have many teachers you didn't like? I've had two out of six so far. Did you enjoy school? I do sometimes. There is a girl in my class that speaks only Spanish. Her name is Jorgelina. She comes from Argentina.

I hope you get this letter. Do you know that I saved ten letters from you?

Love,

Hope

September 10, 1987

Dear Hope,

I am sure that you are delighted to be back in school. It is wonderful that you have a girl in your class who speaks only Spanish. It would be even more wonderful if, while she is learning how to speak English, the children in your class would learn Spanish from hearing her speak. If her mother is as wise as mine was, she would tell her to speak only Spanish at home. In that way, she won't forget how to speak her native language.

Mamma insisted on our speaking Yiddish when we spoke to her. Now your great-aunt Sarah and I are grateful to her, because we can speak Yiddish to each other. We children thought Mamma was the most intelligent woman in the world, and also the bravest. She seemed absolutely fearless.

One bitterly cold night in January, the snow was piled deep, and the wind was howling. It was about nine o'clock, and Mamma said that we should get to bed. Just then we heard a noise in the cellar. (In the olden days, nobody spoke of a basement.) Rosie, Harry and I stood absolutely still, as if rooted to the spot.

Mamma said, in Yiddish, "It sounds as if somebody is moving around down there."

We begged her to get the police. But Mamma didn't listen to us. We had gaslight, but Mamma still had an oil lamp handy. She lit it, opened the cellar door, and called down in her broken English, "Vat you doing down dere in my cellar?"

Peering out from behind Mamma, we could see what seemed to us to be a huge man at the bottom of the stairs.

He said, "Please, ma'am, it's awful cold outside. Let me stay here. I don't mean you no harm."

Without a moment's hesitation, Mamma said, "You hungry?"

The man said that he was. Mamma closed the door. There was no food left from dinner, but she did have bread. She sliced almost half a loaf and buttered the slices thickly. On two slices she put cheese, and on two more some jelly. She heated up a pot of coffee and poured out a large, steaming cup. All this she quickly placed on a tray. Then she opened the cellar door and called out, "Here. Coffee and food. You eat now."

Our uninvited guest walked up the steps. Rosie, Harry and I were speechless with fear. All the man said was, "God bless you, ma'am." And he walked down with the food.

Mamma called after him, "Dere is qvilt down dere on shelf. Keep you varm. But don't touch nutting else!"

The next morning the man was gone. Everything was where it belonged, and he had even folded the quilt. Mamma spent the day at her store feeling unhappy that he had left without breakfast!

Even today, I marvel at her courage.

Love,

Grandma

Please, ma'am, it's awful cold outside.

September 15, 1987

Dear Grandma,

Why did your mother let that man stay and not call the police? What did you think? Jorgelina is *mean*. Do you know what she does? She steps on everybody's feet and punches them in the stomach! I liked your story.

Love,

Hope

September 20, 1987

Dear Hope,

As soon as an adult sees what Jorgelina is doing, she will stop. Only animals act that way.

I don't wonder that you are surprised that Mamma did not get the police. To understand it completely, you would have to know Mamma. She was the kindest person in the world. She had seen a human being in need. It was bitter cold and getting colder. He would have frozen to death if he had left the house. Mamma wouldn't have put a dog out on such a night. And as for me, if Mamma thought the man should stay, then that was the right thing to do. I suppose that Rosie and Harry must have felt the same way.

The other day I was thinking of my brother. We were always close, but after Sophie and Sarah were married we grew even closer. We had such good times together. When it came to inventing games, nobody could match Harry. He could make *anything*—and did!

One day after school just he and I were at home. He said, "Let's play William Tell." He had just read the story of William Tell. It's about a man who meets the demand of an evil ruler. He must shoot an apple off the head of his own son with a bow and arrow. In that way, he would win the freedom of the Swiss people.

Harry made a bow and arrow. That wasn't easy to do, but he did it. Of course, he never intended to shoot it off *my* head. He was much too smart to do that! He put a pile of books on the kitchen table, a glass milk bottle on top of the books, and on top of the milk bottle he put an apple. He backed up almost to the end of the kitchen, and on the second try he hit the apple. Then he gave the bow and arrow to me.

On the very first try the arrow flew not through the apple, but through the china cabinet that had glass doors! The glass and several cups splintered. Both of us were horrified.

Just then Sophie came in. She was horrified, too. She turned to me and said, "It's a good thing that you didn't aim it so Harry would have been hit instead of the cabinet!"

Then Harry said, "Hilda didn't 'realasize' that you have to aim before you shoot."

Ever after we always said 'realasize' instead of 'realize' to remind us of that day—but only to one another, of course!

Love,

Grandma

When it came to inventing games, nobody could match Harry.

September 24, 1987

Dear Grandma,

That was a great story! Please write back *very* soon so I can have the whole story in my book of your letters. It is better than any other storybook because the stories are true. Yours are more interesting stories, anyway. I think my favorite one is about your childhood, but they're all *great*.

Love,

Hope

September 30, 1987

Dear Hope,

It is strange, I have written you so many stories about my childhood, but I never did write you about the first week of my life.

I was the least-wanted baby in the world. A week before my birth Mamma's youngest child—a beautiful little blond boy—died. Mamma was heartbroken. When Mamma was told that the new baby was a girl, she turned her face to the wall. In an Orthodox Jewish family, a boy ranked much higher than a girl. Perhaps she would have felt the same even if I had been a boy, but the fact remained that Mamma was depressed, and nothing that Papa or anybody said about the new baby lightened her spirits. Poor Papa was beside himself. Mamma was always so cheerful, so full of laughter—the life of any party.

Then Papa had a brilliant idea; he would give a party. I was born on the third day of Sukkot. Papa—with the help of all his neighbor's teenage sons—had built a sukkah, as he did every year. (Papa did the directing. The boys did the building!) As is proper, the top of the sukkah had widely spaced slats, and all the slats were covered with branches full of leaves. The inside was decorated with fruits and some grain. An Italian man who owned a fruit store had sent in a bushel of his finest fruits, and his sons, the neighbor boys, and Sophie and Sarah hung apples, oranges, grapes and pears from the sweet-smelling ceiling.

On the last day of Sukkot Papa surprised Mamma by bringing home everyone who was at the synagogue that day. The woman who cared for Mamma had been told in advance to prepare for the party. She had baked and baked. Mamma, of course, had been told nothing. About an hour before the party was to begin, the woman told Mamma to hurry and dress because Papa was bringing home guests.

Once everyone was there the excitement of being the center of attention, and of hearing the baby admired, had just the effect on Mamma that Papa had hoped it would. She took a good look at me and decided that I really looked quite precious.

Years later, when Mamma and I were battling the Depression, I helped her out of a particularly bad spot. She turned to me and said in Yiddish, "Look at this. You were the baby I wanted the least. Yet you are the child who is my greatest source of comfort." I have never forgotten that moment.

Love,
Grandma

On the last day of Sukkot...

October 6, 1987

Dear Grandma,

    I don't understand why a boy would be more
important than a girl. It doesn't seem right. All children
should be loved the same. Did everyone feel that way
when you were growing up? Please write more about
your childhood.

Love,

Hope

Dear Hope,

I couldn't agree with you more. There is *definitely* no reason why a boy should be valued more than a girl in any family. What is really strange is that although we girls knew that Mamma favored Harry because he was her only son, it never bothered us at all. I suppose it was because we all felt loved and secure that we didn't begrudge Harry his special place in Mamma's heart. In my next letter I'll tell you an interesting story about Harry, but right now I would like to give you a clearer picture of what life was like for a child growing up in the early 1900s in a big city.

My earliest memories are of living in a very small apartment (we called them "flats") on a block with huge buildings surrounding a brick yard a block square. Nowadays these buildings would be called tenements. As I recall, every flat usually had about three or four rooms and had no fewer than five children. *All* of the adults were immigrants who came over with only the things they could carry. But *all* of them had dreams of what their children were going to accomplish in this land of limitless possibilities.

The adults had a terrible time earning enough to pay for those tiny rooms in which they lived, but the children who were too young to work had a wonderful time. All of them played on the brick yard in the back. They played ball, with a ball made of rags and a bat made out of the fallen limb of a tree, or a rail from a discarded banister. Some of the girls jumped rope, with the experts jumping "Double Dutch," with two girls turning two ropes at the same time, and one girl jumping over *both*! Now and then a mother would call out for her children to come in and practice the violin or piano. Yes, even in such poverty, immigrant parents who did not know how they were going to pay their rent paid for music lessons *first*. Mamma—like me—had a horror of being in debt, so there were no music lessons for us.

A friend with whom I grew up tells this story about her husband Herman, who grew up to be a pharmacist. His mother had visions of his becoming a noted violinist, even though he had *no* ear for music. She took him to the leading violinist of St. Louis. The lessons cost $1.00 each. In those days, $1.00 would have bought ten loaves of bread.

One day, when the mother paid Mr. Brant the $1.00, he said, "Mrs. Spivack, your son has no ear for music. You are wasting your dollar."

"Am I getting seventy-five cents worth?" she asked.

"No", he answered.

"Fifty cents worth?"

"No", he said firmly.

"Well," she continued almost pleadingly, "twenty-five cents worth?"

This he could not stand. "Twenty-five cents worth you are getting."

"Then," she said happily, "seventy-five cents a week will be my extravagance."

So Herman continued taking lessons, even though his mother often went without an adequate dinner. He did not become a violinist, but he learned to play well enough to teach both of his sons. Was the immigrant mother right? Who knows?

I seem to have gotten away from my description of my childhood just a bit. The streets of the city were unpaved. I believe they were cobblestones. On the way home from school Harry and I would stop at the blacksmith's shop and watch him put horseshoes on the horses. If he had time, he would make rings for us. By that time a crowd of about twenty children would have gathered. The blacksmith would heat a nail until it was red-hot, twist it into a ring, and when it cooled he would see which child the ring fitted. One day, to my delight, a ring fitted *me*! He stopped and asked me what my name was. When I told him it was Hilda, he took back the ring, heated it slightly, and carved the letter "H" on it. My happiness cannot be described.

Years later, when I taught English in the fifth grade and the children studied "The Village Blacksmith," I told them this story. They loved it, but they could not imagine St. Louis with a blacksmith, or, for that matter, even with horses on the streets. That is how much the city changed while I was growing up.

Love,

Grandma

Years later, when I taught English....

October 15, 1987

Dear Grandma,

Here's a poem I wrote. I won second prize in a Tri Kappa poetry contest. It's called "Visions of the Future."

Sometime in the future,
A time that may never be,
No war, no destruction,
Just freedom and peace.

The paper that I am writing on is sixty-eight years old! It is parchment. Daddy and Mama gave me a writing case that belonged to Daddy's grandfather. He never used the paper, so I have it now. It came with a little dictionary, an address book, and a little book that says notes on it. Unfortunately, the envelopes are not quite the right size, but I am trying to use them. Please write the story about when your mother couldn't find her money and thought Uncle Harry took it and found out it had fallen into a drawer. I wish you could come soon.

Love,

Hope

October 19, 1987

Dear Hope,

Thank you so much for sending me a copy of "Visions of the Future" with your poem in it. It is truly wonderful that your poem was chosen to be included.

There must have been a great many poems submitted—considering how many schools there are in Lafayette, so you should be proud.

I promised you a story about my brother Harry, and here it is. I already wrote you about the special place my brother had in Mamma's heart, and that we didn't mind at all. Mamma was a *wonderful* mother. She was lenient with us, up to a point. That point was honesty, truth, kindness to each other and to all people. Those were the qualities she demanded in us.

Anyway, every night, usually after we were in bed, Mamma counted the money she had brought home from her business. The change she stacked in piles of ten: ten silver dollars, ten half dollars, and so on. One night, for some reason, only Rosie and I were in bed while Mamma and Harry were in the kitchen. She was almost through stacking the change when she thought she heard a knock at the front door. She left the kitchen for a few moments, and when she returned she found two half dollars missing. She was positive that she had counted each stack correctly. So when she found only eight half dollars instead of ten, she asked Harry if he had touched the money. Again and again she asked, and again and again he insisted that he hadn't even been near the table.

They searched the floor. Mamma examined her pockets to see if the coins had dropped into one of them when she got up from the table. She knew that they could not have disappeared by themselves. The only explanation left was that Harry had taken them and lied to her. She felt that in some way she had failed as a parent by being too lenient. She had not stressed truth and honesty enough. So she did what she never before had done with any of us—and what she never again did. She whipped Harry. He went to bed crying, and insisting that he had not even been anywhere near the money.

Mamma was terribly upset, so as soon as she finished counting she decided to make herself a cup of tea to calm her nerves. She opened the drawer of the table to get a spoon, and there were two half dollars. If she and Harry hadn't been so upset, they would have noticed that the drawer was slightly open! The money had simply slipped into the drawer when Mamma had gotten up to see if someone was at the door.

Mamma was heartsick to think that she had doubted the word of any one of her children. Harry was asleep, and Mamma didn't have the heart to awaken him. So she went to bed crying and didn't sleep a wink that night. The first thing in the morning she hugged him, she kissed him, and she apologized to him. But still, her failure to trust him haunted her so that she even mentioned it long after I was a parent.

Years later Harry came to visit your grandpa and me. When I told him how distressed Mamma had been even years and years after it had happened, he didn't even remember it!

Love,

Grandma

October 25, 1987

Dear Grandma,

I liked the story about Uncle Harry, but how could he forget about it? I couldn't. Could you?

Please write the story about the white blouse that burned and how your sister bought you a wool dress. Here is some more parchment. Isn't it nice? When my writing desk was new Calvin Coolidge was president.

Love,

Hope

October 28, 1987

Dear Hope,

I *thought* you would like the story about Harry—even though it is rather sad when you come to think about it. I, too, was surprised that he had forgotten the incident. I can't imagine *ever* forgetting something like that. Anyway, now I feel that I owe you a happy story. On the whole, we children had what we needed. But one winter money was really scarce, and we knew it. We always knew when not to ask for anything that we could not eat, and that winter was one of those times. Unfortunately, I found myself with only one white blouse and one dark blue pleated skirt. Naturally, a white blouse could only be worn one day. So my sister Rosie washed the blouse every night and put it on the radiator to dry. In the morning she would iron it.

One morning, to our dismay, the radiator left stripes of rust on the back of the blouse. There was nothing to do but to wear it as it was! Although it was winter, the rooms at school were warm. I was too embarrassed to let the other children see those stripes, so I left my coat on. The teacher, of course, asked me why I was wearing my coat. I told her that I was cold. She sent me to the nurse, thinking that I must be sick. The nurse knew at once that I did not have a temperature. So back I went and hung up my coat with the rest of the coats. It wasn't a good feeling. Rosie and I never did tell Mamma about the incident. We loved her too much to make her unhappy.

Fortunately for me, Rosie had found work in a department store, and that very day was her first payday. She knew exactly what she was going to do with her money. That same evening she and I went to a store, where she bought me a *beautiful* wool dress. It was navy blue plaid with a pleated skirt, and it was trimmed with a navy blue collar and cuffs. Around the waist was a wide navy blue belt. To this day, whenever I see a dress or skirt made of navy blue plaid, I think of the generous thing Rosie did in giving me the very first money that she had ever earned. It all seems so far away, and yet it is all so vivid.

Love,

Grandma

...she bought me a beautiful wool dress.

November 1, 1987

Dear Grandma,

I got my ears pierced the week before last. I have three pairs of earrings. I will buy more soon. Please send the story about how you and grandpa met. I have 13 letters from you! My book of letters is getting very fat.

Love,

Hope

November 5, 1987

Dear Hope,

If you like earrings, you were wise to have your ears
pierced. I can't wait to see how you look in earrings.
When I was born, every baby girl had her ears pierced a
few days after she was born. The strange thing is that I
don't recall ever wearing pierced earrings when I was a
child. Nor do I remember my sisters or any of my friends
wearing them either.

You asked when I first met your grandpa. It was at the
wedding of my sister Sarah. Your grandpa was Sarah's
husband Jake's younger brother, but he seemed more
like a grown man to me. I was about eleven, and he was
nineteen. We barely noticed one another then. I was
much more interested in the beautiful dress that Sarah
had made for me to wear. The night before her wedding
she had gone to a party her friends had given for her.
She came home late, but she stayed up until almost
daybreak finishing my dress. I can still picture it. The
dress was made of sheer white organdy over a pale pink
slip. It had a long waist attached to a short skirt which
was the fashion in those days. A wide pink satin ribbon

went around the waist, and the ribbon was tied in a huge bow at the back. I felt like a bride myself!

It wasn't until two years later that I saw your grandpa again. He was living with Sarah and Jake by that time, and they had invited me to spend the summer with them. (That was the summer that I ate all five pounds of peanut butter!) Anyway, this time I couldn't help noticing him. He looked very tall to me because I was so short. He had the most beautiful black curly hair and enormous brown eyes. He was very popular with the young ladies, as you might imagine.

Grandpa teased me whenever he got a chance. We always did the dinner dishes together. I would wash and he would wipe. He would call me "Hilder" just to get me angry. Finally Sarah came to my rescue. One morning when your grandpa was away, I complained to her, and she said, "Don't show any anger. Just call him Samuel with the emphasis on *muel*. That will stop him. He hates the name Samuel and wants to be called only Sam."

That night grandpa and I were doing the dishes as usual. When he said "Hilder," I sweetly said, "Yes, Samuel," and really put the emphasis on the *muel* part. He never said "Hilder" again.

I didn't see him again until I was a young lady. Then, whenever he would come to St. Louis for a visit, we would go out for dinner and dancing. He was a wonderful dancer and had a lovely manner about him.

On one of Grandpa's visits he asked me to marry him, and I said, "Yes." I couldn't have said "yes" to a finer person.

Love,

Grandma

I couldn't have said "yes" to a finer person.

November 9, 1987

Dear Grandma,

I wonder where Grandpa got the name Hilder. It certainly sounds strange! It snowed today. We have about an inch and are expecting more. When I was in school we had a tiny blizzard. Unfortunately, it stopped after five minutes. Having snow is fun! Did you get any?

Love,

Hope

November 13, 1987

Dear Hope,

I forgot to write in my last letter that I now have fifteen letters from you. I have saved every one of them in a box!

This week I have been giving my apartment a thorough cleaning, and it reminded me of a story I don't think I have sent you yet. I wrote you in another story about my sister Sophie's rule: "A place for everything and everything in its place." After Sophie and Sarah were married, and we younger children were old enough to look after ourselves, Mamma had the same rule. If we forgot and left our things out, Mamma would remind us once or twice. *But,* Mamma had her limits. Mostly we children recognized when those limits had been reached, and we were careful not to step beyond them. I was about fifteen when I failed to anticipate just how far I could go.

I learned how to type the first year I went to high school, and that was lucky because I then had a way to earn my spending money for the next seven years. At the beginning of my second year in high school my English teacher asked if anybody could do some typing for him. He was writing a book. The work would have to be done at home. I was the only one who volunteered, because I was probably the only one who had a typewriter. My brother Harry had bought a new Underwood—the finest typewriter of that day.

Dr. Stratton, the teacher, liked my typing so well that he recommended me to two members of the St. Louis Authors Society. Their name was Farnham, and I was to stop by their house after school, which I did. Mrs. Farnham handed me a short story that she needed to have typed right away. She was certain that it was perfect as it was, but still she wanted a chance to go over it. Could I have it done in about three days?

I hurried home. We had a living room table that was oblong. It was a beautiful table when it was uncluttered, but since I had started my typing business it was *never* uncluttered. Mamma had asked me several times to put everything away before I went to bed, because she didn't like to start the day by walking into such a disorderly living room. I should have realized that Mamma had reached the end of her patience.

I typed until late that night, long after everybody was in bed. I intended to get up very early and continue, but I overslept. When I awoke, Mamma was already up and saying her morning prayers. I rushed into the living room and saw that the table was cleared of everything but the typewriter. I dashed into the kitchen, and although I knew the rule about not interrupting Mamma when she was praying, I asked her two or three times, "Mamma, where are all the papers that were on the table?" Finally she pointed to the bucket of coal. There I saw the rumpled papers with which Mamma had wiped the top of the kitchen stove before starting a fire. I smoothed out those papers—the original papers that Mrs. Farnham had handed me so lovingly—and *whole pieces* were missing. I was too stunned to say one word. I sat down at the typewriter and pieced the story together as well as I could. Fortunately, I could still make out most of it. But how could a fifteen-year-old possibly match a gifted adult when it came to writing? I did my best, however, and I was able to finish the story on time.

When I returned the typed sheets of "Mr. Prouty's Strange Dream" to Mrs. Farnham she took one look at it and said, "Where is the original?"

"Oh," I answered innocently, "I didn't know you wanted it back."

"Yes. I always want it back. This doesn't look like what I wrote. Hereafter you must always bring the original back!"

Why she gave me a second chance, I will never know. But she did. This time she rewrote it, and I was careful to clear the table every night before I went to bed. "Mr. Prouty's Strange Dream" won a prize in a national contest for the best short story written by a first-time author!

I must tell you that I learned my lesson well; a lesson that has held all these years. Even when I am not feeling well, before I go to bed, I try to put everything where it belongs.

In all fairness to Mamma, she did not know how important those papers were. I still think she was the most wonderful woman who ever lived. She loved her children, and she wanted them to grow up properly.

In my next letter I'll tell you about a time that I was *too* neat.

Love,

Grandma

My brother Harry had bought a new Underwood...

November 16, 1987

Dear Grandma,

I liked your story. It was a really good one, but how could your mother throw away your papers? She didn't even ask you!

Please write about how you were too neat. How can you be too neat?

Love,

Hope

November 20, 1987

Dear Hope,

I can understand your surprise that Mamma would actually throw my papers away, but I truly feel that I deserved it. It is not as if she didn't tell me more than once to put my things away. Mamma worked hard all of her life to take care of us. She always made us feel loved and secure. I can't fault her for losing her temper and taking action. It was certainly a lesson well learned for me!

How can someone be *too* neat? I thought that would interest you! It happened one afternoon when I was about fourteen. I was alone in the house and had nothing special to do. So I decided to clean out a trunk which held ever so many of my personal things. They were things that I had started to make and never finished, like clay dolls, pieces of doll furniture made of toothpicks and straw, and other similar projects. Each thing was wrapped in newspaper so it wouldn't break. The trunk was also a place for me to keep newspaper articles I wanted to save, as well as bits of material to sew doll clothes. The whole effect when you looked into the trunk was that it was filled with rubbish.

Mamma had been after me for weeks to go through the things. She told me to save what was important to me and to burn the rest in our kitchen stove. I decided that this was the time to do it. I opened one crumpled piece of newspaper, nothing important. I threw it into the stove, and I opened another. Again, nothing important. Into the stove it went. At this rate, I would be here all day! Finally, after unwrapping two more papers and tossing them into the stove, I simply threw all the remaining papers into the fire *without looking*! When nothing was left, I was satisfied and went over to the store to tell Mamma.

When there was a lull between customers, Mamma asked whether I had locked the door carefully.

I said, "Of course I locked the door carefully. I *always* lock the door carefully."

"I wanted to know because I hid all of yesterday's and today's receipts from the store in your trunk. I wrapped the money in newspapers so that nobody who might break into the house would recognize that there was money in that pile of rubbish."

I almost fainted. I don't know how Mamma managed it, but we children always had what we needed. However, there was definitely no money to burn! When

I told Mamma what I had done, *she* nearly fainted. How was she going to pay her bills? There was no time for her to think about it, because customers walked into the store, and she had to go about her business as if nothing had happened. I walked home feeling miserable.

Later that night Harry asked Mamma, "How much cash was there? The checks will be no loss, because your customers know you well enough to give you duplicates."

Mamma said, "Eighty-nine dollars."

Harry said, "I'll give you the eighty-nine dollars, and I don't want one word ever said to Hilda about the money again. It was an accident."

Even today eighty-nine dollars is a lot of money, but in 1916 it was a small fortune to us. When it came to family loyalty, Harry couldn't be matched. He didn't want me to suffer by being reminded of what I had done. Neither did he want Mamma to be worried about the money. I never forgot what Harry did for me—and I never will.

So, Hope, that is how a person can be *too* neat. If all goes well, I should be there in Lafayette in time for Thanksgiving. I can't wait!!

Love,

Grandma

November 24,1987

Dear Grandma,

Why didn't you look before you threw everything
away? You were fooled just the way any robber that
broke into the house was supposed to.

I can't wait till you come. It's almost Thanksgiving!

Your pen pal,

Hope

Dear Hope,

I loved every minute of my visit. It was wonderful being with my family and sharing Thanksgiving festivities. Thank you for helping to make my stay in Lafayette so special.

The last story I wrote you was about my brother coming to my rescue when I accidentally burned the money that Mamma had hidden in my trunk. So it is fitting that I write about what happened just a few months later.

One morning Mamma asked me to deposit the last few days' receipts in her bank account as soon as I got home from school. I promised that I would. She showed me where the money was hidden and told me to be extremely careful. Harry (being older than I was) usually took care of depositing the money.

When I arrived home I forgot all about my promise and started to study for an English exam. When Mamma came home that night she asked whether I had deposited the money. Of course I had to tell her that I had forgotten. I felt terrible, because I knew the importance of getting the money into the bank as soon as possible to keep it safe. I told Mamma that I would take care of it the first thing in the morning.

You may be sure that I was at the bank at eight o'clock in the morning. To my surprise, there was a long line there already—almost to the corner! I got in, and before I knew it the line extended halfway around the block. People were talking—and talking angrily. I finally asked the man ahead of me if there was always such a crowd in the morning.

He said, "Haven't you heard? The bank has closed its doors. Nobody can get a cent out of it until the books have been examined. We're hoping that if there are enough of us, and we get angry enough, we can get part of our money out now."

I was bewildered. "Was the bank open yesterday?" I asked.

"Yes", he said. "And many of these people standing here deposited money just yesterday. Nobody had an inkling about anything being wrong with the books."

I said nothing but hurried home. I knew I would be late for class, but I could not take several hundred dollars to school with me. When I told Mamma, she was stunned.

She said in Yiddish, "The Lord performs in mysterious ways. He made it so that Harry was too busy to go to the bank, and you were too busy studying to remember that you had promised to deposit the money. If Harry had gone to the bank as usual, or if you had remembered to deposit the money, I don't know what I would have done about paying my bills. I don't know where I would have turned."

Then Mamma kissed me and told me I was her blessing. I can still see her as if it were yesterday.

Love,

Grandma

December 10, 1987

Dear Grandma,

Thank you for the "gelt" for Hanukkah. Mama and Daddy bought me a ballet skirt. It is light purple with dark flowers. Yesterday school was closed because it was 49 below zero (wind chill)! It was the last day of school for two weeks anyway, and it would have been a pizza party. Ugh! I hate pizza parties! When you were little, did you have a three-month summer vacation?

Was that the beginning of the Depression? I read a book called *Heidi*, and her grandmother said that when you pray, the Lord gives you what you want at a better time. If Heidi had gone home when she wished, Clara would never have been able to visit her. So it was better that the bank closed. Have a happy Hanukkah!

Your pen pal,

Hope

P.S. I loved your visit.

December 19, 1987

Dear Hope,

The closing of our bank had nothing at all to do with the
Depression. It was *years* before the Depression, and we
had never heard of a bank closing its doors. If the
examiners had not checked the books at that time, the
bank would perhaps have solved its problems. In fact,
had the bank settled with its depositors, everyone would
have gotten ninety percent of their money. *But,* the state
of Missouri sent in its own examiners, and by the time
they finished there was little money left because the
examiners themselves fled with most of the money! So
seven or eight years later, each depositor received only
about twenty percent of his money. Mamma had very
little in her checking account, but Harry had about eight
hundred dollars, which was a tremendous sum in 1916,
when I was fourteen years old. In the end, Harry
received only about one hundred and sixty dollars! Such
a thing could not happen now if you deal with a United
States government insured bank. The government
promises to repay each dollar!

I am happy that you enjoyed the Ḥanukkah money I sent. You know, Hope, money has always been the traditional gift for Ḥanukkah. Oh the fun we children had with our Ḥanukkah "gelt", as we call it in Yiddish. For hours we discussed what to buy with so much money, a whole quarter! Harry always spent only part of his gelt. Rosie and I spent *all* of it. But the fun the three of us had even thinking about all the things we *could* buy. Even today, Ḥanukkah is a warm time for families—and a quarter is still special to me! Have fun with your "gelt"!!

Love,

Grandma

It was years before the Depression, and we had never heard of a bank closing its doors.

December 23, 1987

Dear Grandma,

Did you notice that we keep sending each other the same stamps a lot? I love your story story. It is *great*! I kept the <u>H</u>anukkah card you sent me also because it has a really good story in it. I put it in the book with letters. It is a big book because I have almost a half a year's worth of your letters! That's a lot!

Love,

Hope

January 1, 1988

Dear Hope,

You are right. We have been pen pals for over half a year. It makes me so happy to know that you are enjoying it as much as I am. You have rolled the years back for me, and I have thought of people and events that I thought I had long forgotten. I do thank you for that.

I have another correspondent whom I don't believe I have mentioned to you. My oldest sister Sophie's daughter Rosalie and I exchange letters, although not as frequently as you and I do. Yesterday I received a letter from her reminding me of something I am sure I never told you.

It was about 1917 or 1918 when a terrible influenza epidemic struck St. Louis. All of the schools were closed for weeks, and all public meetings were canceled. None of the so-called "miracle drugs" had been invented, so doctors had very little with which to combat influenza. Everywhere people were dying. The very young and the very old were especially hard hit.

One day, to our horror, Sophie sent word that both children (Rosalie and her younger brother Paul) had been ill for two days, and now she and her husband Sam had gotten up with high temperatures and were too weak to move. As if that weren't enough, they were almost out of food.

Poor Mamma was beside herself. She *had* to go to the store. There was no one she could pay to help Sophie and her family, because people were afraid to enter *any* home where there was influenza for fear of catching it themselves. With terror in her heart, and with a fervent prayer, Mamma sent Rosie and me with a freshly baked hallah and a basket filled with chicken, carrots, celery, and a large onion: the makings of chicken soup. That was Mamma's cure for *anything* that was wrong with you.

Once we arrived there we soothed the children, changed the sheets on everybody's beds, saw to it that every member of the family took some liquids to bring down the fever, and began to prepare the soup in a huge pot on top of the stove. Then, as Mamma had instructed us, we took the baby's empty buggy and a long shopping list and loaded up on food.

For ten days we took care of them. Sophie never forgot it. Everyone in her family recovered, and believe it or not, neither Rosie nor I got so much as a sniffle!

A year or so later there was another epidemic. This time Mamma was ill. She allowed herself only four days in bed. Then back to the store she went. Again, Rosie, Harry and I emerged unscathed. The Good Lord was watching over Mamma and her brood. That's how Mamma always thought of it.

Love,

Grandma

January 9, 1988

Dear Grandma,

I am surprised that your mother sent you and Rosie to Aunt Sophie's house. You said in your letter that everyone was afraid to go into the house other than their own. I am surprised that you and Aunt Rosie didn't get terribly sick. I'm glad that you didn't. Was influenza just the flu? I thought it was a serious disease.

I hope you had a *happy* new year. We made decorations and put them all over the playroom. I made a paper chain and a big snowflake. I also made a paper chain and snowflakes for my doll.

Love,

Hope

Dear Hope,

You are not the only one who is surprised that Mamma would send two of her children into a house with influenza. As a mother, I, myself, have difficulty imagining how I could take such a risk with a child of my own. But Mamma felt that she had no choice. Who else was there to help Sophie and her little children? I can only think that it was Mamma's deep faith in the goodness of God that gave her the strength to make her decision. Even though it is difficult for me to understand, I have never questioned the wisdom of her choice.

Yesterday I was reading an article in the newspaper about the Great Depression. I don't think I ever mentioned to you that your Grandpa and I became engaged officially not too long before the stock market crash of 1929. I know that I wrote you about how we became reacquainted after we were both adults, and how he asked me to marry him on one of his visits to St. Louis, and how I accepted him. I was a schoolteacher then, and your Grandpa and his brother Jake had three service station supply businesses in and around

Pittsburgh, Pennsylvania. Today they would call them gas station supply businesses. They sold everything that the stations would need—except the gas!

One Labor Day weekend I visited Sarah and Jake in Pittsburgh. Of course, I saw a lot of your grandpa as well. On my first night there Grandpa and I went for a ride. It was quite late when we stopped in Schenley Park. Grandpa turned off the lights of his car, and both of us looked at the moon. It was almost full. Grandpa said, "Isn't the moon beautiful, and isn't the night wonderful?"

Then he put one arm around me, and he kissed me. A second later, when I looked down, there on my finger was the most beautiful ring. I hadn't even felt it when Grandpa put it on! It was platinum, with a large diamond in the center. On each side was a row of three small diamonds, then two, and then one. I loved it! Years later I read in the newspaper that the older son of President Calvin Coolidge had given his fiancée an exact duplicate of the ring that Grandpa had given me!

Grandpa gave me the ring at exactly the right time. He had sold some stock to buy it. In the fall of that year the stock market crashed, and the crash was felt around the world. Overnight, Grandpa's stock was almost worthless. Only by that time he had very few shares left. He sold most of it to buy my ring!

Let me know if you are interested in the Great Depression, because I can think of several stories concerning its effect on us directly.

Love,

Grandma

One Labor Day weekend...

January 19, 1988

Dear Grandma,

Our teacher told us about the Depression last week. I told him you were alive then and you were a teacher, too.

I do want to hear your stories. I bet they are better than his!

Love,

Hope

January 23, 1988

Dear Hope,

This is really a remarkable coincidence. You just happen to be studying the Great Depression in school when I offer to share some of my stories from that period in history with you. Do any of the other children have grandparents who remember that time? Probably not, but still, you never know. You might just ask them.

As I wrote, had Grandpa waited only two months to sell his stock, I never would have gotten an engagement ring. And while a ring is not a necessity for a happy marriage, it is nice to own one.

The crash of the stock market was felt by everybody, rich and poor alike. Teachers fared the best, at least in St. Louis they did. Our salaries dropped about ten percent in actual cash, but the cost of living fell about fifty percent or more! So we were actually ahead.

At home I was the only one who really earned money. Mamma's business dropped drastically. My brother Harry, who was unable to find work of any kind, finally rented a part of a friend's store and opened a small printing shop. It barely paid for itself. Rosie stayed at home and took care of things there. Summers were always hard, because, as you know, teachers do not work during the summer months. During the Depression they were even harder. But somehow we managed.

In Pittsburgh, where my sister Sarah, her husband and their two children lived, along with your grandpa, things were worse. All of the steel mills, which used to operate twenty-four hours a day, were either closed or operating about ten hours a day. That affected *every* business. And Grandpa's was no exception. Two of the businesses closed within two years. Only the one in a small town called Wilmerding was left. Sarah's husband Jake took all of the merchandise that was left from the two stores and kept it at home. Each day he would put some items in his car and sell them directly to service stations. Grandpa managed the one store in Wilmerding himself. In that way they managed to eke out a small living for themselves.

At the Ashland School in St. Louis, where I taught, although the teachers did not suffer, their families and the families of their students did. One twelve-year-old boy in my homeroom fell asleep as soon as he sat down. It happened so many times that I asked him to bring his mother to school. A week later his mother came. She said that Phillip was falling asleep because he simply did not get enough food. Her husband was unemployed, and they were trying to get along on with what little money was left—hoping that he would find work. She apologized for not coming to school immediately, because she didn't have a pair of shoes to wear. I looked down, and she was wearing a brand new pair. She had scraped together a dollar and bought them.

I was heartsick. I told our principal, Mr. Short. He called a dairy, who agreed to supply them with milk, butter, cheese and eggs. Then he called a wholesale baker, who said they could have day-old bread. Next he called a wholesale grocer, who said that he could spare a few cases of canned goods. Last on Mr. Short's list was a wholesale meat packer, who sent them some meat. By the time Mr. Short had completed his calls they were so well supplied that they were able to help some of their neighbors. Mr. Short, however, had not quite finished. He sent home letters to all the parents asking them to please send all of the *good* clothes their children had outgrown. He called an emergency meeting of all teachers, asking them to be on the alert for other children who might be undernourished or poorly clothed.

I write all of this to give you a picture of why your grandpa and I (who loved each other dearly) could not get married before 1936, when things finally looked a little brighter. Not that everything about the Depression was so grim. In my next letter I'll tell you about a cheap form of entertainment that took St. Louis by storm.

Love,

Grandma

The crash of the stock market was felt by everybody, rich and poor alike.

January 28, 1988

Dear Grandma,

It is very cold where we are. Is it hot in your area?
What is your favorite kind of weather? Mine is cold and
snow. Please write and tell me what happened to Phillip
and his family. Is the gold ring Mama had engraved for
me your high school or college ring?

Love,

Hope

Dear Hope,

As a matter of fact, I *do* know what happened to Phillip's family. His father got an interview with the president of a manufacturing company and offered to sell their products on a commission basis only. That means that he would not receive any salary from the company. He would only receive a set percentage of whatever he sold. Very soon he was making enough money to support his family. That was one story that had a happy ending. Things didn't always turn out so well for other families during the Depression.

In my last letter I promised you a story about the roller skating fad that hit St. Louis. People, whole families, looked for things to do that would break the tension of everyday living, things that did not require money. They brought up skates that were lying in the basement unused, oiled them, polished them, put them on and took to the streets. In fact, after seven o'clock in the evening, certain streets were closed to traffic by the police just for the skaters.

One morning before school opened two teachers came into my classroom and told me about the fun they had the night before when they decided to join the skaters. They invited me to come along with them that evening. I explained that I had never owned a pair of skates, and that I had no sense of balance, and that I had better not try it. Both of them were expert skaters and assured me that I would be able to learn within five minutes. "Even three-year-olds are skating after just a bit of instruction from their parents," they assured me. "Just be careful to buy a pair of good skates."

I bought the best: $3.25! They were firm, they were strong, they were everything that would make a graceful skater out of a non-skater. That evening, for the first time in my life, I was out on skates, supported on each side by my faithful Ashland School colleagues.

I soon discovered that fear is a very powerful thing, and I was afraid. It was the same two nights, three nights, four nights. The minute they loosened their grip on me, down I went. But they still kept at it.

The rest of the skaters, of course, were having a marvelous time. They were singing the song made popular by the famed radio and vaudeville singing-dancing comedian Eddie Cantor:

Potatoes are cheaper
Tomatoes are cheaper
Now's the time to fall in love...

I don't recall the rest of the words, but I still hear the happy voices all around me. Everybody forgot their tensions. Everybody was shedding their worries. *Everybody* but your grandma!

That night, as I lay in bed, I came to terms with myself. I was simply afraid, afraid that if I fell one more time, I would break a leg. And then what would happen to me and to my family? At that time in St. Louis teachers did not have insurance for illness and accidents as they do now. They were allowed only three days' sickness, and they received only *half pay*! I just couldn't take such a risk.

The next morning I firmly told Minna and Jean that I was grateful to them for the experience, and especially for their love and patience, but I had better not take any more chances.

That evening the *St. Louis Post-Dispatch* carried this headline:

HOSPITAL EMERGENCY ROOMS PACKED
MORE FRACTURES SET IN SIX NIGHTS THAN IN SIX MONTHS

I knew I had made the right decision. I took the skates across the street to the Foundling Home, where they doubtless were put to much better use.

Love,

Grandma

P.S. That was my high school ring. I hope you enjoy it as much as I did.

February 7, 1988

Dear Grandma,

That was a good story about the skating. I know just
how you felt. Everybody I know could skate a long time
ago. Leah showed me how to do it, but it took a long
time. It took the whole summer! I'm glad I can skate,
but it's too cold outside to skate now. Is it cold in
Pittsburgh?

Love,

Hope

Dear Hope,

I am certain that you *do* understand how I felt if it took you months to learn how to skate. Leah must be a very patient teacher, and you must be a very persistent pupil! You must understand, though, that learning to skate when you are nine and learning to skate when you are almost thirty are two very different matters. I am happy that you fared better than I did!

It is so cold in Pittsburgh today that I am simply staying inside. The temperature has been below zero for the past few days, which reminds me of a story that happened on my last Sunday as a Sunday School teacher—just before I was married. I may not have mentioned to you that in addition to teaching school I taught classes every Sunday at a temple not too far from where we lived. The temple was in a very, *very* wealthy neighborhood. Many of the children were chauffeur-driven, and the clothes they wore were exquisite. Well, on this bitter cold Sunday the children had all left the room to go home. After a few minutes a little girl came in and said:

"Miss Abramson, my coat is gone."

"Oh," I answered, "it's out there. I'll help you find it."

But there were very few coats hanging on the hooks. Most of the children had gone home already, and the coats still hanging there clearly belonged to boys. So I called the head of the department, a lady my age in years, but twenty years older in her thinking. She looked all around, and said—very seriously—"Little girl, are you sure you *wore* a coat?"

By that time three teachers were out there, and all three of us burst into hysterical laughter. We couldn't have helped ourselves if our lives depended on it. Even at noon, the thermometer had reached the high of *eight below zero!*

Love,

Grandma

I taught classes every Sunday at a temple...

February 15, 1988

Dear Grandma,

Do you think it was better to be a child when you were young than it is now? I would like to be a child in the early 1900s to find out what it was like and also to ride in wagons and buggies. I rode in a buggy once in San Francisco. Did you ever? We laughed when we read your story. Did the little girl ever find her coat?

Love,

Hope

February 20, 1988

Dear Hope,

As far as I know, the little girl's coat was never returned. Her parents had to replace it.

You asked me a fascinating question, and I have been thinking about it for days. Do I think it was better to be a child when I was young than it is today? I haven't done any research on the subject, but I would say the answer depends on whether you were a boy or a girl, whether you were rich or poor, whether you lived in the city or on a farm, and whether you were the oldest or the youngest child in your family.

When I was young, families were larger. Of course, we didn't have much money, and so much was expected of the older children—especially the girls. There were no labor-saving devices like washing machines, dryers and central heating, so the work of keeping a house was hard. With Mamma away, much too much was expected of poor Sophie. Fortunately, she was blessed with a sunny disposition. She could get fun out of *anything*. But she worked hard—and so did Sarah—and she must have remembered it, because she always said to her daughter, Rosalie, "Have fun while you are young."

While Sophie and Sarah were home, we three younger children lived comparatively carefree lives, but still we were expected to take care of our own things. It is true that we had very few material things, which made it easier to take care of them, but take care of them we did.

There are certainly more hazards today than when I was a child, but there are so many advances in science and in *everything* that I personally feel that it is far better to be a child today. So many things are available to almost everybody that weren't even in existence when I was a child. We didn't have radios. We didn't have televisions. I felt as if I were flying when a neighbor invited me to ride in her electric phaeton when I was about fourteen. It was just like a closed-in carriage, with a battery instead of a motor I guess. It had shades trimmed with fringes on every window, and little draperies. It went about ten miles an hour. Contrast that with your flying to California last summer!

I will say that I would love to know what people fifty years from now will have that we don't have. We have made incredible advances in my four-score-plus years. What will they have then?

Love,
Grandma

HILDA ABRAMSON HURWITZ was an English teacher, and very active in Jewish organizational life in Pittsburgh, Pennsylvania.

HOPE R. WASBURN is a high school student and a former National Spelling Bee contestant. She wants to be a lawyer when she is older.

MARA H. WASBURN is Director of Development and Alumni Relations for the School of Nursing at Purdue University.

Photo Credits

Cover photo of Hilda Abramson was taken by Jacob M. Hurwitz.

Page 8: Hope Wasburn, taken by Leah H. Wasburn, 1988.

Page 11: Harry and Hilda Abramson, taken by Jacob M. Hurwitz, 1910.

Page 15: Sophie and Sarah Abramson, studio portrait, photographer unknown, 1910.

Page 19: Child with fireworks and American flag, July 1906, The Bettmann Archive.

Page 23: Frieda Abramson, taken by Paul D. Hurwitz, c.1930.

Page 27: Montgomery Ward Catalog, Spring/Summer 1934, Missouri Historical Society.

Page 31: Hilda Abramson, taken by Jacob M. Hurwitz, 1915.

Page 39: Man with junked car in empty lot, taken by Ralph A. Ross, 1931, Missouri Historical Society.

Page 43: Harry Abramson, taken by Jacob M. Hurwitz, 1910.

Page 47: Sukkot 1908, 92nd Street YM-YWHA Archives, New York.

Page 53: Hilda Abramson, studio portrait by Sid Whiting, 1924.

Page 61: Hilda Abramson, taken by Jacob M. Hurwitz, 1913.

Page 65: Sam Hurwitz, photographer unknown, c. 1925.

Page 71: Bessie Friedman, a contender for World's Typist Championship, The Bettmann Archive

Page 83: Depositers herded into lines by police, 1924, UPI/Bettmann Newsphotos

Page 91: Sarah and Jacob Hurwitz at Creve Coeur Lake, photographer unknown, 1912.

Page 97: Depression Relief, W.C. Persons, Missouri Historical Society, 1919.

Page 105: First Hebrew Congregation Sunday School, San Leandro, CA, Western Jewish History Center/Judah L. Magnes Museum, Berkeley, CA.